GMAIL MANUAL FOR SENIORS

Simplified Email Guide for Beginners

Peter T. Maxwell

Copyright© 2019

All rights reserved

No part of this book should be reproduced, edited, duplicated or resold without the prior notice of the author.

LEGAL NOTICE

If any individual goes against the copyright act, appropriate measures would be taken thereafter.

Dedicated

To BROWN, our lovely dog

Acknowledgment

I want to say a very big thank you to Martha Maxwell, my wife, for her support.

Table of Contents

Chapter 1
Gmail, king of webmail

Gmail is the world's electronic mail service of choice, riding higher than any other web-based email exchange. Since April 1, 2004, when its beta version was launched, this free mail service created by Google LLC, has grown in leaps and bounds, grossing 1.5 billion average monthly users in 2018. This accounted for 21 percent of the global email market. And the growth is far from cooling off.

The Gmail statistics is just awesome:

- Some 1.5 billion active monthly users as of 2018. And, you expect the number to have grown in 2019.

- The average Gmail inbox contained 17,000 electronic messages

- 27 percent of those creating new webmail addresses are doing so on the Gmail platform.

- Among those aged 18 to 29, male or female, 61 percent of them have Gmail addresses, some more than one.

- 92 percent of start-up businesses in the US use Gmail

- In the case of mid-sized companies, 60 percent of them in America use Gmail.

- In all, 54 percent of webmail users aged 30 to 44 years, use Gmail, compared to 23 percent who prefer Yahoo.

And how do most people access their Gmail? You can trust it's on hand-held devices. Records show that 75 percent of Gmail users send and receive their emails on mobile devices, mostly on Android and iOS smartphones and tablets.

Google, on its part, has surpassed expectations in meeting the needs of a hugely popular and fast-growing webmail system. Besides the addition of several products and innovations to enhance user satisfaction, the Google Company has made Gmail available in

75 languages, assessable to nearly all internet users on earth.

Google has also introduced handwriting features so that languages with special needs can be fully supported to compose emails that meet their needs.

In fact, for now, it's hard to imagine a world without Gmail. And, it isn't hard to figure out why this webmail service is so popular. Consider the following:

· Gmail is free, easy to install and user-friendly.

· It's been generally adjudged safe. Gmail uses automated machine learning (ML) tool, to trap over 10 million spams and malware emails per minute, an amazing tech feat that protects 1.5 billion email address owners

·   A single Gmail account connects you to Google's world of endless digital possibilities

·   Google assigns 15 GB of Cloud storage to each email user, enough to store prized digital assets for a lifetime

·   Gmail account serves as your key to unlocking several third party internet services like *Facebook*, *Instagram*, *Whatsapp*, *Linked-In*, *Payoneer*, *Amazon*, and whatnot.

Chapter 2
How to use Gmail

If you've had a Gmail address for some time, you need to give some thoughts to how you've been using the service. Perhaps, there are steps you can take to enhance your user experience. For instance, some long-time Gmail users aren't aware they can now enable the webmail in the Dark Mode, that is, if they use devices that run on the most recent Android Q version, released by Google on November 4, 2019.

Enable the Dark Mode on Gmail mobile app

- Open your Gmail app,

- Click the three-line menu icon

- Scroll down to **Settings** >> **theme**. There are two options, besides the system default.

- Choose light, dark or System default.

You see, Gmail is in such a state of flux that nobody can claim to have mastered all the tricks. For instance, before now, Google ran a Gmail Lab, where it constantly test-run new ways of enhancing functionality on its popular webmail app. Some users were still searching Gmail Labs when the feature had been renamed **Advanced** in the Settings page.

It's here under the **Advanced tab** that you can enable/disable add-ons like auto-advance, canned response template, custom keyboard shortcuts, right side chat, multiple inboxes, etc., so you can use Gmail like a pro that you ought to be.

Google is constantly adding and removing features under this tab. So, some things you add today may well not be there tomorrow. But Gmail remains the king of webmail, a title it richly deserves.

And if you're a young adult, or anyone else wishing to join the exciting world of Gmail, you need to learn a few simple tricks to help you step forward with your best foot. For the sake of newbies, it makes sense to start the Gmail expose from its logical beginning, which is, creating a Google account.

How to create a Google account

To own Google-based webmail, you've got to create a Google account. The moment you locate the gmail.com website, you'll be redirected to a page where you'll need to sign up for a Google account.

· Locate **www.gmail.com** using your favorite browser. It's good you browse with Google's in-house browser, Chrome, for a seamless interface with other Google products like *YouTube, Maps, Calendar, Drive, Contacts, Google Docs* and so on

·   Choose **create account** at the bottom of page

·   Then tap **Next** to continue

·   On the sign-up form that opens, enter your first and last name and choose a username. If the username is not available, Google will suggest available variations. Select any one of them, or modify the first one you suggested, perhaps, by adding a number, until the system accepts it.

·   Next, fill in your phone number. Google will send a verification code of six numbers, through a text message to the phone number you listed.

- Enter the code in the field provided to complete your account verification.

- You'll now proceed to fill in other personal details, like your date of birth and gender. You'll see the option to provide a recovery email address, which may be useful when fixing any problem that may arise on your new Gmail address. This is optional.

- You'll then have the opportunity to review and accept Google's Terms of Service and Privacy Policy. After you click, **I agree**, your account creation is complete.

A note of warning on password creation

As part of your Google account creation, you formed a password to be used in gaining access to your account. You did well if you made an effort to create a strong password. It enhances your protection as per the safety of your personal information and your security of your digital web assets.

Experience has shown that many do not give much thought to the strength of their digital passwords. For instance, in 2014 September, 5 million Gmail login passwords leaked onto a cryptocurrency forum in Russia. A close examination of the leaked passcodes revealed shocking facts.

For example, it was discovered that only 1 percent of the passwords were considered strong. They contained a combination of letters, numbers and symbols. Ninety-nine percent were classified as unsafe.

Some passwords were as weak as *123456 or abcdef.* The most common ones were words in lowercase like QWERTY, dragon, welcome, and password. Only 42.5 of the leaked login passwords contained a simple combination of letters and numbers, in the form of **abc123**, which even an amateur hacker can easily guess right, to gain illegal entry to your account.

So, there's an evident risk to your digital and financial assets.

You do not want to lose things to hackers. So, take the time to create a password that offers real security to your Gmail account. Make it a minimum of 8 characters, containing a mix of letters, numbers and symbols.

Do not make it too complex that it becomes perpetually hard to remember. Also, write it down somewhere, to minimize the chances of forgetting your password soon after you created it. Seek the help of Password Manager.

Again, it's advisable to change your Gmail password regularly. It's easy to do:

· On your open Gmail page, tap the cog icon

· Scroll down to Settings

· Go to Security settings in your Google account

· Surf the security tab until you see Signing in to Google

· You'd see the section for Password, from where you can see when last you changed yours; and enable 2-step verification if you want.

You'll have to enter your password anew, to confirm your identity. Then, you'll be prompted to enter your new password. As we said earlier, you shouldn't be afraid to create a complex password, for fear you may forget it. You can write it down in a secure place, or use an online Password Manager for support.

After you've entered the new password twice, for confirmation, you'll be alerted if your password change had been successful. You may wish to use the opportunity to look over other account security details like your 2-step verification, recovery email address and phone number.

Signing In and Out of your Google account

If you signed out after creating your Google account, how do you sign in again, when you're ready to use the email system? It's easy.

- Go to gmail.com

- Enter your username

- Also, type in your password

- Click Log in

With a functional Google account, you've got access to a dozen Google services in the digital space. But, since you're interested only in the Gmail service, for now, you can go ahead to download the Gmail app, with an orange-colored M icon. You get this free from the Google Play store.

Although you can use any browser of your choice, accessing Gmail with Google Chrome browser will enhance your Gmail user experience in many ways.

Yea, Gmail is optimized for other notable browsers like Apple's Safari, Window's Internet Explorer and Firefox. But I've never imagined using anything other than Chrome browser to access it. When you open Gmail on Google Chrome, you get a complete package, as it brings you face to face with other Google products.

With the Gmail app on your home screen or desktop, gaining access to your emails is made easy. You just launch the app, and pronto, your mails are in front of you. Like other webmail services, Gmail has a feature that allows you to import contacts from your phone to populate your email address book.

How to add email contacts

Over time, Gmail will help populate your address book and even help you locate whoever you wish to exchange mails with from your address book. For a start, you've got to build up your address book from your phone contacts.

·   On our Gmail home page, click on Google apps

- From the menu of apps that shows up, **select Contacts**

- And from the screen that appears, tap on **Add new contact**

- You should now enter relevant information about the contact in the appropriate spaces

- Tap **Save** to complete

Over time, as you keep sending and receiving emails, Google mail will help you populate your address book, for free. Just as it helps you call up the names when you need to send them emails, with a slight suggestion from you.

Know your Gmail app version

Like all others, the Gmail app comes in different versions, some designed by third-party app developers to support extra features.

While you definitely would prefer the official Gmail app deployed by Google LLC, you should also know that even the official app customizes in three different ways on Android smartphones and tablets; personal computers and laptops; and on iPhone and iPads. Across these devices, you can also view your emails in the HTML mode, if you ever want to do that. The app will display differently in HTML mode.

Although 75 percent of Gmail users access webmail through smartphones and tablets, some Gmail features do not work on handheld devices. For instance, the real-time chat mode and the custom keyboard shortcut feature cannot work on the Gmail mobile app. Also, you may need a PC to effect some of the customizations you'd like to use on the mobile app.

Monetization of Gmail assets

Some experts suggest that the average Gmail account was worth $3,588 as of 2018. The calculation was based on the number of emails in the accounts, and the time it took to write them, and what it will take to rewrite them in case they're lost or damaged. You may then want to know if Gmail account holders can monetize their digital assets.

The answer, right away, is no. Your Gmail system is not money-making. Instead, it provides you with a world-class mail exchange platform, for which you should even pay to use. But Google allows you free use of its global mail service, largely because your presence on the platform makes advertisers want to pay to reach you.

Lately, some app designers have tinkered with the idea of helping users monetize their Gmail inbox. Earn.com is one such app that claimed they can enable users to bounce back promotional messages and adverts to their senders. You then allow them to send you paid messages if they see you as a good prospect for the promotion of their products or services.

And whether they pay or not to resend the message, by bouncing their messages back to them in real time, you free yourself from having to sort through and, perhaps, respond to tons of unsolicited promotional messages.

You've not, as yet, seen many users monetizing their Gmail inbox. This does not mean there're no opportunities to make good money on the web through Google. Indeed, there are many opportunities for skilled web content creators, like yours truly, the author of this manual.

If you can create something of interest to others, be it texts, pictures or videos, you sure have chances of earning decent incomes via Google, with AdSense and YouTube Partner Programs, for successful bloggers and YouTube pro.

Back to Gmail. What you can do for now is to optimize your user experience by using the mail service like a pro. And that's what you'll do if you walk through this manual and make an effort to do what you learn.

Chapter 3
How to customize your Gmail inbox

If you have been using Gmail on hand-held Android devices, you may have been stuck with the default inbox mode. This arranges your emails according to timelines, with the newest emails on top. This is fine in letting you know the age and relative timeline of your mails.

The downside is, placing all the mails on timeliness tends to accord equal relevance to all of them. In reality, the emails don't have an equal value to you. You're bombarded with tons of messages (the Gmail average is 121 per day), the majority of which are irrelevant. Yet, you've got the unenviable task of sifting through much chaff to find one useful grain.

To help you organize your emails, Gmail automatically sorts them into five broad categories or tabs using their algorithm. The categories are Primary, Social, Promotions, Updates and Forums. You tap on any of the tabs to see what messages Google has filtered in there.

Gmail hasn't given much public explanation about how it sorts mails into the five categories. But when you look at the type of emails in each category, you'd see a clear picture:

· **Primary**: You'd readily see that mails in this category came from persons on your contact list or address book. They could be friends, family members, and colleagues at work, or anyone else with whom you've exchanged emails before.

· **Promotions**: These are emails offering you something special, something to buy on discount, or telling you to do one thing or the other, for personal or corporate benefits. They usually come from stores, shopping carts or marketing agencies.

· **Social**: Messages or notifications from social networks like Facebook Twitter; sharing sites YouTube and Instagram; websites for dating and gaming portals are usually filtered into this category

· **Updates**: This category will hold messages from your service providers, including internet-based firms and utility companies. Mails having to do bills, receipts and alerts will usually land into this group.

· **Forums:** Gmail will use its algorithm to filter notification emails from any forums or discussion groups you may belong.

Neither the sender nor you, as the receiver, can determine how Gmail classifies an email. But you can easily move the mails from one category to another if you want.

- On your Android phone or tablet, open the Gmail app

- Tap the icon standing by the mail you want to reclassify

- Tap the three-dot icon at to the left of your view

- On the options that open, tap Move to

- On the new view, tap the category you want to relocate the mail to

When the email moves, you'll be given some seconds to decide whether to undo the move, in which case the mail will revert to its original category. On a PC, you can drag the mail to where you want it to be, or even create a keyboard shortcut for this function.

How to customize your Gmail inbox layout

Even when your mails are sorted into five categories, you still have the challenge of having every mail in a timeline, with the latest mails staying on top. On Android phones and Tablets, you have room to tweak your inbox layout to achieve a different outcome, like keeping the more important mails on top.

This is how you can tweak your Gmail inbox layout:

· On your smart device, open the Gmail app

· Tap the three-line menu icon, top left of the home page

· Choose Settings

· Select your account

· Choose Inbox Type

· Tap any inbox type among the options of **Important first, Priority first, Unread first, or Starred first**.

However, other than the Default inbox, only two or just one other inbox option deserves your consideration: the **Important first** and perhaps, the **Unread first**. And why should we not bother about the other types? Well, the difference between important emails and priority mails is just a matter of semantics. And if you use starring to show that a mail is important to you, you're still saying that the starred mails are of priority importance.

Even, you might as well forget about the **Unread first** inbox type. There isn't much sense in retaining unread stories at the top of your mails, when those stories weren't read, probably, because you did not consider them worth reading.

However, if you're in the habit of marking important stories as Unread, even after reading them (perhaps because you intend to return to them later), then you can enable the Unread first inbox type. This means that messages you've not read will stay on top of your inbox, followed by newer emails that haven't also been read.

You're then left with **Important first** as the only inbox type option, aside from the Default setting. Let's take a look at it.

Important first Gmail inbox type

It's Gmail's wisdom that determines which of your emails qualify as important, or deserve priority status, and should rank above the rest in your inbox. But they're gracious enough to explain the factors they use to judge the importance of your messages.

For instance, Gmail will automatically take as important:

·   Emails from contacts you exchange mails frequently

·   Which emails you open as soon as they come in

·   Which mails you ended up replying to or forwarded

·   The keywords in the emails you always read

·   How you treated the mails, whether you deleted, snoozed, archived or starred them

Any emails that match their expectations will come with the importance marker symbol and stay on top of your inbox if the inbox is configured to **Important first** setting. You can click on the symbol to change the status if an email turns out not to be that important to you. You can also hide the symbol.

How to hide the importance marker symbol

You can hide the importance marker icon if you hate to see it. But you can't do so on the mobile app.

· On your PC, click on the Gmail app page

· At the top right corner, click on **Settings**

· Select Inbox tabs

·　　On the Importance markers area, click **No markers**

·　　Look down the bottom of the page, click **Save Changes** to hide the importance marker symbols.

The changes you made on the PC will synchronize on your Gmail mobile app and show it on your smartphone or tablet.

How to hide or show in-boxes and labels on the home page

On your android smartphone and tablet, all the Gmail inbox icons and labels are lined up vertically on the left edge of the screen. While handling a mail in the default inbox mode, the screen is split in two, showing all the icons and labels on the left. Your emails occupy the right half of the display or screen.

If you hide them, you'll get additional display space for your messages. And it's damn easy to hide them while reading your emails and return to them when you need to.

·   If the labels are hidden, tap the three-line menu icon located top left of the screen.

·   The screen splits into two showing inbox icons, labels and everything else on the left edge

· Tap again on the menu, and watch the labels return to hiding, giving way for more email display.

You have much leeway to make your Gmail inbox and mail format look and feel unique. One option you have, and which you will like to try, is to download Gmail Email Template, a Chrome browser extension.

With that custom template, you'll find many things you can tweak to make your mails identify you, or your business name. For instance, your mails can bear your digital signature, your picture, or your company logo, all downloaded and embedded in the email template.

Notes about snoozing, archiving or deleting emails on Gmail

After you've read emails, there are a whole of things you can do, if you do not just want to leave the mail in the inbox. You can snooze, archive or delete them.

When you snooze an email, you wave it aside for now, because you think it's not something you want to handle at the moment. You can tell Gmail when you'd like to treat it, and it will reappear then for your attention.

It's different from archiving the mail, which implies you don't need the email now, but might need at some point in time. Archiving moves mail away from your inbox but it definitely remains part of your **All mails collections.**

But when you decide that an email is not needed now, and you're sure it will never be needed in the future, you delete it. Deleting takes it into Trash, where it will stay for 30 days, and vanish permanently. Within the waiting period, you can restore it to the inbox. But you always empty your trash at any time you want, not waiting 30 days for waste to disappear automatically.

Chapter 4
How to send and un-send emails on Gmail mobile app

It's time to start sending emails. In this manual, we'd assume you're among the majority of Gmail users who access the webmail on Android mobile devices. Even if you have been doing this for a long while, you can still go through the procedure, if only for the fun of it. Who knows, you may just see a couple of ways to optimize your Gmail user experience.

· On your smartphone or tablet, launch the Gmail mobile app

· Tap the Compose icon represented by a **plus sign (+)** at the bottom of page

· In the **To** space, enter primary recipient of your mail

· If more people need to be in the loop, copy them in the **Cc** space

· You can even blind copy more people in the 'Bcc' field. Your primary recipient and those directly copied, will not be aware you copied those in the Bcc field.

· Then fill in the Subject of your mail

· And proceed to write what you have to tell your mail recipients.

When you're done composing an email, take some moments to read through what you've just written. Read slowly, and pay attention to each word, so you do not read what's on your mind as if it's what you've written down.

Many email writers do not spend time to edit their mails. How often did you post an update on the social media platform, or send a mail to your contacts, only to realize, a few moments afterward, that the post or mail was full of flips and flops?

Sometimes, the errors are so intolerable that you're left with no choice than to delete the update, or recall the mail. You can avoid all that pain, by just taking a few moments to spellcheck, and read through what you've just composed.

The system can help you to spellcheck your email messages. When you finish composing, look at the bottom right of the page, click on the **three-dot icon**, **More** and select **Check spelling**.

If you use Gmail on a PC at school, for work or in any organizational setup, there's a feature that can automatically fix misspelled words. To autocorrect your mails:

· Click Settings in the top right corner

- Select General

- Enable **Autocorrect**

Each word that's autocorrected will carry a temporary line under it. If you think the correction is inappropriate, you can click undo, to retain the original word, or type in the correct word by yourself.

In all, your slogan should be: any unedited text is not worth posting or sending. Unfortunately, sloppy writing seems to be in vogue, with many young adults not giving a damn about spellings and rules of grammar! You don't want to join the millennial carelessness.

Undo a Sent mail

If you write carefully and spend a few moments to refine your emails, you'll rarely have the need to undo what you've just sent. But again, textual errors aren't the only reason you might want to take back a sent email. What if you sent the email to the wrong persons, or you circulated a message ahead of its due time? You'll certainly want to recall the email.

Before now, Gmail users needed to enable the Unsend feature to enjoy the service. It now functions in default. But you can customize it, especially on the PC. For instance, you can increase the time you have to decide whether to recall the mail you just sent. If you customize it on the computer, it'll function on your mobile app when you sign in with the same Gmail account.

What you need to do is:

- Open your Gmail app and tap the **cog icon**

- Select the Settings menu, where you'll find all kinds of features you can adjust to your taste

- Reach down the General tab and locate **Undo** Send

- Here, you'd find the option to tweak the Send cancellation period

- You can choose a minimum of 5 seconds, then in multiples of five, up to a maximum of 30 seconds to be able to cancel the email you just sent.

In case you ever need to undo a recently sent email, remember this:

· Soon after you send a mail on Gmail, you see Sent

· You also see the option to Undo the sent message. Depending on your settings, you can have a window of 30 seconds to undo a sent email.

· Just tap Undo to cancel the message

It's good to note that the email you sent will definitely hit the inboxes of people you addressed it to, even during the cancellation window. Some recipients may have even started to read your mail if they're online and consider your mail that much important. Clicking your undo option will make the mail disappear from everyone's inbox.

How to reply to messages on Gmail

Replying to emails isn't any different from writing new emails. You can limit your reply to the one who sent the mail to you or rely to all persons copied.

· On your Android device, launch your Gmail app

· Open the mail you want to reply to

· At lower part of the message, you'll see three bars, Reply, Reply All and Forward

· Tap Reply or Reply all, if that is what you want to do

Gmail may suggest a phrase to you, taken from the mail you're responding. Simply tap on the phrase to begin composing your response. Remember to edit your reply message, just as you do on everything you intend to send out.

How to turn off Gmail nudges

Granted that you downloaded the updated version of the Gmail app, the new feature called Nudges may be working on your mobile app. It nudges you, or reminds you, to respond to an email you might have missed. And to follow up on a mail you sent but haven't received any response.

You'd see reminders on top of your inbox items, suggesting to you which emails to reply to, or follow up. If you love the new feature, you can let it work for you. Otherwise, you can take short easy steps to hide the nudges.

· Tap the three-line icon on the top left of the screen, and select Settings

· Look at the Nudges section

· Remove the checkmark on Suggest emails to reply to, and Suggest emails to follow up on

How to turn off Gmail Smart Reply

You may also want to turn off the Gmail Smart Reply feature if it's enabled in default. The feature uses some tactics to generate possible responses to your emails. In a way, smart reply functions like the autocorrect tool, this time, not just for individual words, but for the entire mail you want to write.

Normally, you'd see three response options, composed in line with your previous email behavior. It comes handy when you truly want to reply to an email but lack the time, or headspace, to knock it off.

Incidentally, this very important feature is currently only available in the mobile app and does not show up for every email. It appears for shorter mails that pose specific questions, and require a predictable sort of response.

If **smart** reply is on default in your Gmail, you may think you have no need for it, or the response options never really match what you want to say. You can proceed to turn it off, this way:

· Open the Gmail app

· At the top of the page, tap the three-line icon

- Select Settings

- Tap on your Gmail account

- Remove the checkmark in the box next to Smart Reply.

How to schedule your email to send later

There are times you finish preparing an email, but you need to wait for an appropriate time to send it. Using a Gmail scheduling feature, you can set up the mail to be automatically sent for you at the scheduled time.

For email scheduling on Android devices:

- Launch the Gmail app by tapping the icon on your screen

- Tap the compose icon, a Plus (+) sign

- Create the email

- Tap the three-dot icon at the top left corner

- Then, select Schedule send

- Choose one of four options and tap the final Schedule send

There are four options available, namely**, tomorrow morning, tomorrow afternoon, Monday morning and Pick date & time.** If you choose to pick your date and time, you then have a leeway to choose when your email departs from your outbox.

The time may vary in minutes, depending on your time zone.

To view or alter scheduled mails

You can always return to your Scheduled emails to change your schedule, or even cancel it if you change your mind about the mail or the timing of its departure. To do so:

·   On the Gmail app, tap the three-line icon top right

·   Tap Scheduled, then choose the email you want to act on

·   Tap Cancel send. You can stop here if all you to do is to cancel the scheduled email. But if you want to reschedule it for another time,

- Tap the email again and create your changes

- Then, tap the three-dot icon top right

- Select Schedule send and set your new option for sending

- Tap **Schedule send** again, to complete the action.

How to format your emails, choose fonts, colors

Unless you know this trick, you may have no room to format anything in your mail. You see no way out of a monotonous font or a colorless mail. Indeed, Gmail allows adding colors and other varieties to your mail, as you please.

So, you can add bullet points, highlight aspects of your email, underline, embolden and strikethrough aspects of your email.

· On your smartphone or tablet, open Gmail app

· Tap the compose icon, could show as a pen, or plus sign (+)

· Create your message

· Double-tap what you want to format

· Then, select your formatting option like to change the font color, bolding or italics.

Chapter 5
How to add a custom signature to your Gmail

The signature and location address that appears at the end of your emails can add a touch of professionalism to your messages. A standard signature will contain your name, job title, and your contact information, including the URL of your website, if any.

You can include a designer text, a logo or a picture. An effective email signature should help you gain the respect of your client, in addition to the obvious fact of telling the email recipients what you do.

Embedding a custom signature in Gmail isn't rocket science, either on the PC or on the mobile app versions. Signatures created on the PC can synchronize and also show on your Gmail mobile app.

From a PC:

· Open the Gmail app

· Click on the gear icon at the top right corner of the screen, then go to Settings in the drop-down menu

· Under General, locate the Signature area

· Enter your signature text in the field provided. Five lines should take everything necessary in a professional signature, in addition to any image and contact information you may want to include.

· Use the formatting bar to make your text special, or add image

You may not see the formatting bar. Not a big deal. You can start a new message in a rich-text format to enable you to customize your signature the way you want.

When you're done, click **Save changes** to have complete the process. Henceforth, each time you click to compose an email, the signature appears right away, enabling you to tweak it now and then, as you deem necessary.

How to place Gmail above quoted texts when replying mails

It is customary for Gmail to quote the emails you're responding to or forwarding to other recipients. You'd obviously prefer your custom signature to come immediately after your response, and not after a long chain of quoted text.

To determine where your signature is placed:

· On the Gmail app, click the cog icon

· Choose Settings in the drop-down menu

· Then, scroll down to General tab, then Signature

Just below the signature field, you'd see a box where you can put a checkmark. As you do that, you commit Gmail, always to insert your signature before quoted texts when replying, and to remove quotation marks in the line preceding your signature.

How to include a picture in your Gmail signature

Earlier in this section, you heard that including a picture in your email signature might be very helpful in boosting your image among clients, among other benefits. If you haven't added a picture or any other illustration in your email signature, the idea of doing so may sound scary.

But, again, this isn't anything near climbing Mount Everest.

Instead, it is just as easy as selecting a good picture from your digital photo gallery and placing it in your Gmail app, after a couple of clicks.

This is how simple it is:

·   On your Gmail app, click the cog gear icon and go to Settings

·   Your General tab may be highlighted in default. Otherwise, choose it.

·   Get down to the signature area

· Place your cursor where you want the picture or image to appear and click

· From the signature editor menu, click **Insert image**

· In the **Add image** dialog box that shows up, browse your picture in any of your digital stores. Select the image and click to insert it into your signature area.

If you have issues with the picture's size, you've got the right, and the tools, to resize it. You can choose from three options of small, medium or large. Next, you go down to the bottom of your screen and click on Save

Changes to complete a photo addition to your Gmail signature.

Chapter 6
How to troubleshoot your Gmail

Gmail, in general, rarely encounters a system failure. Since inception in 2004, the webmail has reported only one system outage.

That was in February 2009, when some 100 million Gmail accounts collapsed for 2 hours, 30 minutes. Because it was night across US time zones, most users here were asleep and did not feel the outage. But the extreme slowness that afflicted the system following its restoration was greeted with twitter rage among American clients.

While system collapse is rare, there are times when your Gmail app may refuse to sync. You'll then be faced with problems like:

- Emails are stuck in the send mode

- New mails aren't dropping in your inbox

- You can't open or read emails

- Gmail app is very slow in responding to commands

- Account sync error message keeps showing

There are a few things you can do to fix these problems. After you try each step, try to sync your account and see if the original problem is fixed. Otherwise, try the next step.

Run an update on your app: Missing out on updates will definitely affect the performance of your Gmail app. And if you don't run software updates on your device, even an updated Gmail app may misbehave.

Restart your device: Many app performance issues can be rectified by simply shutting down and restarting your devices. It's one step that you shouldn't ignore if your Gmail account refuses to sync

Check your settings: First of all, you need to ensure your device is connected to wireless network service. If you're not online, you cannot synchronize your accounts. Also, check to see if your airplane mode is turned on and if your Gmail sync settings are all enabled.

Clear your storage: If your device is short of space, syncing won't work well, or won't work at all. So, as part of your troubleshooting effort, try to unclutter your device. The following efforts might free much space in your device and improve its functions:

· Remove apps you don't need, or those you rarely need

· Delete digital downloads and files you created, or move them to an external storage drive

· Relocate music, books, movies or TV shows and audio files you've downloaded from Google play

All of these should free much space on your device and help needed apps to perform better.

Check password: Of course, you cannot sync if you cannot sign in to your Gmail account. In that case, you may be receiving error messages like 'invalid credentials', 'username and password not accepted' or you're repeated prompted to enter username and password.

You can take the following steps:

· Be sure your login information is properly entered

· Try signing in with your app password in place of the regular password, that is, if you enabled two-step verification

· If you can't sign in to Google account despite everything, then seek help from Google Help Center by clicking on issues menu that applies to your case. You'd wait for online help and follow instructions.

ABOUT THE AUTHOR

Peter Maxwell has been a certified apps developer and tech researcher for more than 17 years. Some of his **'how to'** guides have appeared in a handful of international journals and tech blogs.

Printed in Great Britain
by Amazon